WHAT IS
HANUKKAH?

WRITTEN BY
SHARI LAST

FESTIVAL OF LIGHTS

When you think of winter holidays, what comes to mind?

I bet you think about snow, twinkly lights, and lovely warm food, right? Lots of people think about Christmas trees and Father Christmas, too. Well, I'm Jewish, so when it comes to the winter, I don't celebrate Christmas.

But my family and I do celebrate a different holiday — and it also has twinkly lights and lovely warm food. It even involves presents, games, and sometimes parties!

I'M TALKING ABOUT HANUKKAH.

OH, HANUKKAH

Hanukkah is a Hebrew word that literally means "dedication". However, since Jewish people light the Hanukkah candles every night of Hanukkah, it has become known as "The Festival of Lights".

WHEN IS HANUKKAH?

Hannukah begins on the 15th day of the Jewish month of Kislev, and it lasts for eight days.

Did you know that the Jewish holidays are worked out on the lunar calendar? This means they fall at a slightly different time every year. Hannukah can be at any time during November and December.

THE LUNAR CALENDAR

The lunar calendar is based on the cycles of the moon, not the sun – which is what the "regular" calendar is based on.

HANUKKAH
CAN YOU SPELL IT AGAIN?

The spelling of the word "Hanukkah"
is often a cause for confusion!

In Hebrew, it is spelt like this:

חנוכה

In English, many people spell it like I do – Hanukkah –
but I've seen the following spellings as well:

HANUKKA   **CHANUKA**   **HANNUKAH**

CHANUKAH   **HANNUKAH**

There's no right or wrong English spelling,
so don't lose any sleep over it!

LIGHT THE HANUKKIAH

On each night of Hanukkah, Jewish families light the Hanukkiah. This is a candelabra with nine branches — one branch for each day of Hanukkah and a ninth to light the others (known as the shamash).

On the first night, we light one candle. On the second night, we light two — and I'm sure you can work out the rest. The eighth night is my favourite, because the Hanukkiah looks so beautiful all lit up!

DID YOU KNOW?

The Hanukkiah is based on the Menorah, the golden candelabra from the ancient Jewish Temple. The original Menorah, however, had seven branches, plus the shamash.

Some families light one Hanukkiah for the family, while others have a Hanukkiah for each person. At my school, we make a Hanukkiah every year as our Hanukkah craft. Last year, mine was a butterfly!

THE STORY OF HANUKKAH

I bet I can guess your next question:

Why do Jewish people celebrate Hanukkah?

Great question! To answer, let me take you back more than 2,000 years to 164 BCE . . .

The second Jewish Temple stood proud and tall in Jerusalem. However, a Greek Hellenistic king, Antiochus IV, had taken over the Temple and forbidden the Jewish people to practise any part of their religion, under penalty of death.

An old Jewish priest named Mattityahu defied the orders of Antiochus, so becoming the voice of the rebellion. Mattityahu had five sons, and when he died, he urged his sons to continue the fight for Jewish freedom.

Judah the Maccabee was the leader of the five brothers, who all became known as the Maccabees. Together, they led the Jewish rebellion, defeating Antiochus's troops and making their way to Jerusalem to reclaim the Jewish Temple.

THE MEANING OF MACCABEE

The word "Maccabee" might have come from the Greek word for hammer, suggesting that Judah was the hammer of G-d. Some people think the word "Maccabee" is an acronym (the first letter of each word) taken from a Jewish phrase that means "Who is like you among the mighty, God?"

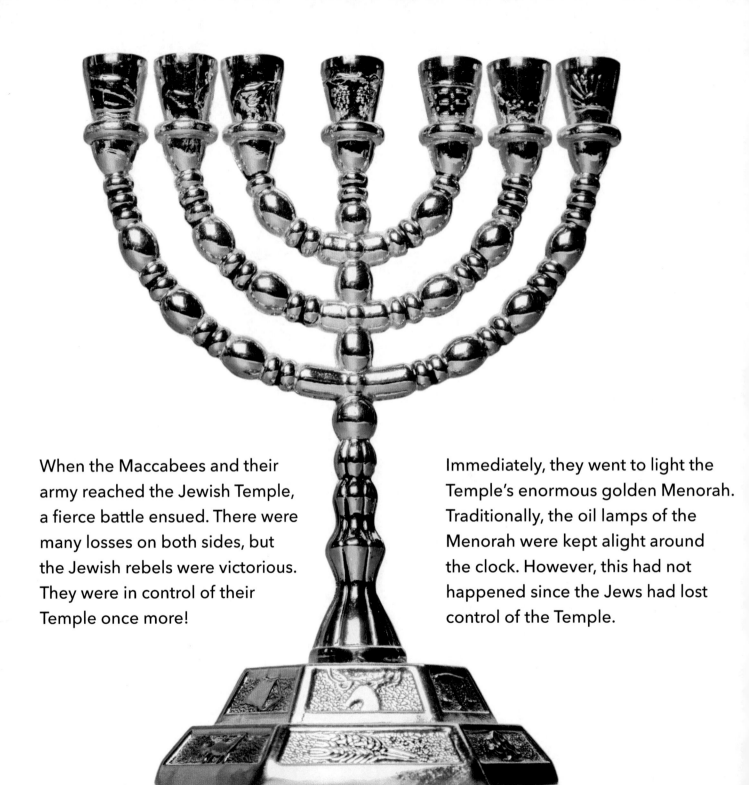

When the Maccabees and their army reached the Jewish Temple, a fierce battle ensued. There were many losses on both sides, but the Jewish rebels were victorious. They were in control of their Temple once more!

Immediately, they went to light the Temple's enormous golden Menorah. Traditionally, the oil lamps of the Menorah were kept alight around the clock. However, this had not happened since the Jews had lost control of the Temple.

The Maccabees were dismayed to see that the Temple had been ransacked and ruined. They feared they wouldn't be able to find any pure oil with which to light the Menorah.

Eventually, they found a small jar, containing enough oil for just one day. But a miracle took place: the oil didn't burn for just one day – it burned for eight whole days!

So that's why we celebrate Hanukkah – because the Jews reclaimed their holy Temple and rededicated it by lighting the Menorah. And that's also why it lasts for eight days – because of the miracle of the oil.

TRADITIONAL FOODS

Speaking of oil, that reminds me of perhaps my favourite Hanukkah tradition: the food!

To remember the miracle of the tiny jug of oil that lasted for eight whole days, Jewish people traditionally eat foods on Hanukkah that are fried or cooked in oil. This includes latkes, which are the most delicious fried potato cakes, and doughnuts, which, as we all know, are cooked in oil.

FRY YOUR OWN

Near the back of this book, there's a recipe for latkes, if you'd like to try making them one day. I like to dip them in apple sauce.

My family has our own Hanukkah tradition – we have a doughnut party on one night of Hanukkah. We buy lots of plain, sugar-covered doughnuts and inject them with our own fillings. Jam is the most traditional, but I like to try different flavours, such as chocolate, caramel, or custard!

OH, DREIDEL!

Hanukkah is a happy festival, when we celebrate the fact that we are free to be Jewish and to practise our religion openly and proudly.

Back in the days of Antiochus, when the Jews weren't allowed to do anything Jewish, they would often meet to study ancient holy texts in secret. If one of Antiochus's guards passed by, they would pretend that they were playing a game with a small spinning toy called a dreidel.

Playing with dreidels on Hanukkah is a way for us remember those difficult times, and to celebrate our freedom now. Plus, it's pretty fun!

THE DREIDEL

"Dreidel" is pronounced like this: *dray-dl*. There is a Hebrew letter on each of its four sides. They represent the Hebrew words that form this phrase: "A great miracle happened there."

PLAY A GAME OF DREIDEL

If you want to have a go at a game of Dreidel, check out the instructions near the back of this book.

HANUKKAH GIFTS

It's become traditional to give Hanukkah gifts, which is a tradition I fully approve of!

Every family is different and has their own way of doing things. Some families give gifts on the first night only, while others give a small gift each night.

I know one family who gives one gift on the first night, two on the second night, three on the third night, and so on. I've done the math: that works out to 36 gifts in total.

AWESOME!

HANUKKAH AROUND THE WORLD

On Hanukkah, Jewish people around the world light their Hanukkiahs and place them by a window in celebration of religious freedom – and to spread the light!

Of course, different countries and cultures have unique Hanukkah traditions. Do you want to find out more?

TUNISIA

Tunisian Jews use the seventh night of Hanukkah to celebrate the heroic women of the Hanukkah story, Yehudit and Chana. This festival-within-a-festival is known as Chag HaBanot (Festival of the Daughters).

AUSTRALIA

When you picture Hanukkah in Australia, don't imagine a snow-covered scene . . . because Hanukkah takes place in the summertime! Hanukkah parties, complete with doughnuts and latkes, are often held in parks or on the beach.

MEXICO

Mexican children play a game called Toma Todo (winner takes all), which is similar to Dreidel, although the dreidel has six sides, not four. Some even celebrate Hanukkah with a dreidel-shaped piñata!

MOROCCO

In Morocco, some families extend Hanukkah to include a ninth day – known as "the day of the shamash". Children go from house to house, collecting spare Hanukkah candles. Then, they light a bonfire and celebrate with singing and dancing.

CUBA

In Cuba, a Hanukkah treat is fried plantain, rather than potato latkes. They are called tostones. To make them, plantains are fried, mashed a bit, and then fried again.

HANUKKAH GREETINGS

I hope you've enjoyed learning about Hanukkah.

If you have any Jewish friends and you want to wish them a happy Hanukkah, here are a few ways to say it:

"HAPPY HANUKKAH!"

"HANUKKAH SAMEACH!"

Pronunciation: *Hun-oo-kuh Sum-ay-uch*
(This means "Happy Hanukkah" in Hebrew)

Note: the "ch" in "Sameach" is a sound you make at the back of your throat. Or you can just use an "h" sound.

"CHAG SAMEACH!"

Pronunciation: *Chuhg Sum-ay-uch*
(This mean "Happy Festival" in Hebrew)

Note: the "ch" in "Chag" and "Sameach" is a guttural sound you make at the back of your throat. Or you can just use an "h" sound.

LET'S MAKE LATKES!

Ingredients

- 2 large potatoes, grated (squeeze out excess liquid)
- 1 onion, grated (squeeze out excess liquid)
- 2 eggs
- 3 tablespoons plain flour
- Salt and pepper
- Vegetable oil for frying

Method

1. Mix all the latke ingredients together with your hands or a spoon.
2. Heat enough vegetable oil to cover the bottom of a pan.
3. Shape the mixture into balls and then flatten them between your hands.
4. Place into the hot oil and fry until golden on both sides – approx. 2 minutes per side.
5. Place on kitchen paper to remove excess oil, then serve.

DIP DILEMMA

What will you dip your latkes in?

They go with anything! Try these dip ideas: apple sauce, sour cream, yoghurt with herbs, sriracha, or even creamy horseradish sauce.

LET'S PLAY DREIDEL!

What you need

- 1 dreidel
- Approximately 100 small items
  (for example: chocolate coins, sweets, marbles)

How to play

1. Divide the small items evenly between each player.
2. Everyone puts one of their items into the middle. This is the "pot". (If the pot is ever empty, each player puts one item in.)
3. Each player takes a turn to spin the dreidel.
4. Depending on the letter visible on top when the dreidel falls, that player does one of the following:

נ	ג	ה	ש
Nun	**Gimmel**	**Hey**	**Shin**
Player does nothing	Player takes the whole pot	Player takes half the pot	Player puts one item into the pot

A player is **out** when they have run out of items. The **winner** is the player who wins all the items, or the player who has the most items when you decide to end the game.

HANUKKAH CRAFT IDEAS

BUILD YOUR OWN HANUKKIAH

You don't have a Hanukkiah? No problem! Think of what you could use to build your own. The eight lights of the Hanukkiah should be on the same level, but the shamash (the candle you will light the others with) can be higher or lower.

DIY HANUKKAH DECORATIONS

Let's get creative! What can you find to create some beautiful Hanukkah decorations? You could use paper, fabric, pom-poms, or even sticks from the garden! How about adding some fairy lights? The sky's the limit!

GET BAKING

Nothing says a Jewish holiday like delicious food, so how about baking Hanukkah biscuits? Perhaps you want to have a go at cutting out festive shapes? Or would you rather use your decorating skills to spell out some Hanukkah greetings with icing?

MAKE PAPER DREIDELS

Get your paper and scissors out and see if you can build your own dreidel. You could even write the correct Hebrew letters on the sides (see the page before this one for a reminder). Use tape to stick the sides together, and then see if your dreidel can spin!

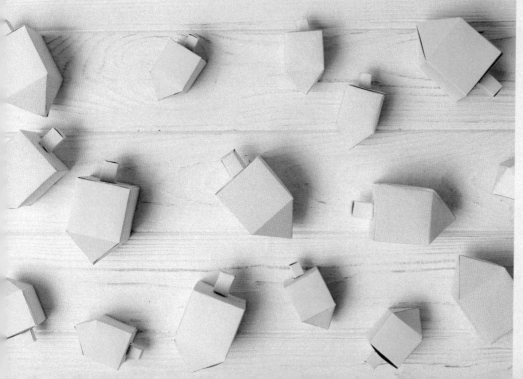

Tell Me More!
NEW IDEAS FOR KIDS

First published in Great Britain in 2021
by *Tell Me More!* Books

Text copyright ©2021 Shari Last
Design copyright ©2021 Shari Last

ISBN: 9798754928121

Picture credits: Thanks to Vecteezy.com, Freepik.com,
Adobe Stock, Pikisuperstar, Sheri Silver, Andrés Goméz,
Roberta Sorge, Ksenia Chernaya, Rodnae Productions,
Ekaterina Molchanova, Marco Brivio, Racool Studio,
Ben White, Kadarius Seegars, PICHA, and Romolo Tavani.

Made in the USA
Las Vegas, NV
27 November 2023